WHEREVER WE ARE WHEN
WE COME TO THE END

Richard Barnett is a poet and a historian. *Seahouses*, his first collection, came out with Valley Press in 2015, and was short-listed for the Poetry Business Prize. He taught the history of science and medicine at Cambridge, UCL, and Oxford for more than a decade, and his history books include *Medical London*, a BBC Radio 4 Book of the Week, and *The Sick Rose*, an international bestseller.

Wherever We Are When We Come To the End

RICHARD BARNETT

Valley Press

First published in 2021 by Valley Press
Woodend, The Crescent, Scarborough, YO11 2PW
www.valleypressuk.com

ISBN 978-1-912436-58-3
Cat. no. VP0179

Cover and text design by Peter Barnfather.

Printed and bound in Great Britain by
Imprint Digital, Upton Pyne, Exeter.

to Lauren Jane Barnett

'[The war] saved my life; I don't know what I'd have done without it.'
– Ludwig Wittgenstein to his nephew

'Jerusalem will be wherever we are when we come to the end.'
– Russell Hoban, *Pilgermann*

1.   Silence is not the end of it.

1.01.   Everything turns, so to speak, on *how* one is silent.

1.011.   Not the silence but what is beneath it, beyond it, within it.
           (As in the Matthew Passion.)

1.1.   Silence is all that is the case.
           Silence is all; that is the case.
           All that is, is silence: the case.

1.11.   Shells pass over in silence.
           (Silence is not stillness.)

1.111.   David falls in silence, over and over.
           (We make to ourselves pictures of facts.)

1.1111.   Silence divides into –
           (This is merely material for a thought.)

We wake up just enough to know that we are dreaming.
My dream body moves, but my real one does not stir.
Again.

I.   The duty of an equation is to draw a picture of the world.

1.01.   To strike a target at range x and altitude y when fired from $(0,0)$ and with initial speed v the required angle(s) of launch θ are:

$$\theta = \arctan\left(\frac{v^2 \pm \sqrt{v^4 - g(gx^2 + 2yv^2)}}{gx}\right)$$

1.02.   The trajectory is the curve described by the centre of gravity of a projectile in flight.
          (There is no need to correct for the curvature or rotation of the Earth.)

1.1.   The duty of artillery in war is to destroy the enemy.
          (Earth and chalk thrown up with epileptic grace.)

1.11.   Destruction being impossible, the artillery will attempt to neutralise the enemy by causing a cessation or at least an abatement of his activity.

1.12.   Fire must be opened as rapidly as possible.

1.121.   If the observer is inattentive or inexperienced, the artillery fires more or less at random, wastes ammunition, is poorly informed, and is not properly responsive to calls made upon it.

1.122.   The observer must function however violent the action.
          (Bombardier LJJ Wittgenstein, Fourth Battery, Fifth Howitzer Regiment, Imperial and Royal Seventh Austro-Hungarian Army.)

1.2.   Report position of shots in direction and height, and convert these to corrections to be applied at the battery.

1.21.   A burst is short or over according as it hides the objective or brings it into relief against the smoke.
          The black smoke available for observation is very fugitive.

1.211.   One in three do not explode, burying themselves merely.
          (Not an event in life, not lived through.)

1.22.   The sharpened pencil tip grazing the paper, a point without dimension, a line without resistance.

1.221.   Scratchy voices screaming from the field telephone.
          (Whoever sings, prays twice.)

1.3.   The grace of duty: I renounce my influence on happenings and
          I am free!
          I am spirit and therefore I am free!

1.31.   Shells fall closer –

                                        I cannot make myself understood.
                                         (This, alas, is how it is.)
                                                      Once more.

1.   Under the form of eternity everything is happening at once.

1.01.   Burnished goldleaf frame, tangled brushstrokes, silverpoint beneath.

1.02.   Crystal spheres, stars scattered like seedcorn.
          Roofs, spires, minarets piled up in tempera.

1.03.   A procession with banners and drums. Landsknechts and
          margraves, ritters, friars, peasants and penitent heretics.

1.04.   Crying and praying and laughing, they are all dying and they go on
          dying and the dead live.

1.041.   Graves gape like cell doors.

1.042.   The unpraised dead, upraised, engrossed, unspeakably gorged, full
          of themselves and what they are becoming.

1.1.   Back from Jerusalem, unwounded, unguilty, the donor kneels
          beside the Virgin.
          (The Virgin loves fools.)

1.11.   His tattered blue field coat scarcely clothing his flesh.

1.12.   Cupped in his hands an offering: a field gun with toy soldiers, cast
          in lead, finger-worn, seamed and blobbed with paint.

1.2.   Hail Mary, full of grace and vengeance.
          (What is looking out through her eyes?)

1.21.   Her blue gown blebbed with sweat and ichor, cradling her broken Jew.

1.3.   She speaks: What is the logical form of this?

                              Forgive me, lady, for I have simplified –

1.4.   The still pool of the morning, the ripples of returning sense.
          Tongue clicking on palate, aching ponderous limbs.
          Blue field coat on the back of the door.
          A form of peace. A resemblance.

1.41.   Lauds in the abbey church, beyond the garden wall.
          Entropy denotes the quantity of disorder in a closed system.
          (How the dead lie, or are recruited, or keep silent.)

1.42.   From what have I been saved? For what?
          Who shall I serve? What work is there for me?

1.421.   A small man, gesturing to nobody, fighting himself to stalemate.

1.422.   The haft of the scythe, hand-smoothed, the curve of the stroke, the
          raking of stalks, their rank injured breath.
          (He came and waited for you.
          He left, but said he'd come again.)

1.43.   I desire mastery and grace, misunderstanding and exile.
          (How little is accomplished when these problems are solved.)

1.44.   In the evening when the garden has been tended I am tired, and
          then I do not feel unhappy.
          I dream at my table, a needle threaded through its own eye.

1.5.   His body, falling endlessly, uncradled.
          I give my life; my life is taken from me.

                    What we can articulate is just what we can bear –

2.   We can foresee only what we ourselves construct.

2.01.   We cannot think anything unlogical, for otherwise we should have
          to think unlogically.
          There can *never* be surprises in logic.

                              In meaning? In memory?

2.011.   An aurora, astonishing and real, blooming in the boreal sky,
          before the war.
          David, slight even in parka and boots, and the immense silence of
          the fjord.

2.0111.　Is it as simple as it seems?

2.0112.　The demand for simple things *is* the demand for definiteness of sense.
　　　　The right names and the right relations. (Right : straight : correct.)

2.012.　Sitting together in my room, my eiderdown on our knees, the
　　　　needle in his long fingers, fixing the eye of a button.

> I tremble when I recall this, as I tremble
> when I walk on virgin snow.

2.1.　Summer concerts at the Palais Wittgenstein, before the war.
　　　A boy in a sailor suit, in a forest of sisters.
　　　Uncle Paul grinning, listening, our father's hard eyes on him.

2.11.　Bulletheaded Hapsburgs, rapier-scarred, iron hair cropped, bowing
　　　from the hips.
　　　Trumpets and drums, sentiment and cruelty. A good war is a
　　　good long war.

2.2.　Pray for the soul of Karl Wittgenstein, steelman and patriarch.
　　　In all things businesslike and dutiful, ignorant and wise.

2.21.　In him the furnaces, the forging presses, the agony of the lathe.
　　　Bone bolted to metal, chilled and shrinking, rivet-punctuated.
　　　The blood's thread, red, the rust dusting barrels and breeches.

2.211.　A monster of precision, supple, fettled, fulfilled.
　　　(The mind is easily misled by superficial resemblances.)

2.22.　Silence on the tip of his tongue, blooming like smoke.
　　　Slow mortification, conscious and guttural. A hard end.
　　　Knotted neck-cords, pain capped in each wheeze.
　　　Hissing through bared teeth: das harte Muss, das harte Muss.

2.3.　The end of the world –

> The end of this world.

2.4.   What has history to do with me?
         (The gravity of the dead world curving our paths.)

2.41.   Two men are fighting; either draw a picture of them fighting and
         say that this is how things are, or draw a picture of them not fighting
         and say that this is how things are not.

2.42.   The picture must now in its turn cast its shadow upon the world.

2.421.   Desks and typewriters. Smoke and high ceilings. Hot still air.
         Quiet swift discussions, unminuted. Decent hesitations.
         Morse keys tutting. The century clearing its throat.

2.422.   Declarations handed from ministry to ministry. Diplomatic
         regrets. Timetables.
         (The object is simple. There is only the obligation of setting
         things in order.)

2.5.   What do I know?

2.51.   I know the world is independent of my will.
         (As for what my will is, I don't know yet.)

2.511.   I know Vienna, neurotic and splendid, all tongues, all peoples.
         I know masks. I know Klimt. I know Mahler.

2.512.   I know England.
         I know kites on the moors above Manchester.
         I know Cambridge, motes of dust in a beam of light.

2.513.   I know Norway, the cabin at the head of the fjord.
         I know the light, the silence, David.

2.514.   I know David, poor thin brave David.
         I know what will be expected of him.
         I know he will volunteer.
         I know I would die beside him.
         I know I will not fight him.

2.52.   As for my duty –

2.521.   I know a philosopher must seek a proper ordering of experience
          and action.
          I know an artilleryman must obey orders and the laws of motion.
          I know a son must serve his father and his fatherland.
          I know an Austrian must love the Emperor.

2.53.   I know we will lose this war – if not this year, next.
          (I am not sure I know the referent of 'we'.)

2.54.   I know all soldiers are brothers.

          Pray for the soul of Johannes Wittgenstein, drowning in Chesapeake Bay;
              of Rudolf Wittgenstein, drinking milk and cyanide in a bar in Berlin;
          of Konrad Wittgenstein, who will shoot himself as the Kaiser's army falls apart.

2.541.   These lost boys, incomplete strangers, bodies heaped up, dead of
          the hard must.
          One who is wise, one who is wicked, one who is simple, and one
          who does not know how to ask.

2.542.   I know the sense of the world must lie outside the world.
          (I know the sense of this is beyond me.)

2.55.   I know the only life that is happy is the life that can renounce the
          amenities of the world.
          (The hard must in me. The portrait of my father.)

2.551.   I know this is intolerable.
          (I know I am intolerable, even to myself.)

                              Something in me is screaming and twisting.
                              Something in me does not care to be loved.

2.6.   I am an exile from all I know.
          I know I must enjoy the seduction.
          (The romance, the necromancer.)

3.   At once everything happens.

3.01.   Roused after midnight, no time to dress, the Russians are upon us!
         (Volunteer LJJ Wittgenstein, His Majesty's Gunboat *Goplana*.)

3.011.   Bare feet, splinters of rain, pressing my body around the
         searchlight.

3.02.   Bullets tear the fabric of the air, crease the deck.
         (Calculate the trajectories and inhabit the space between them.)

3.021.   The beam blinds them as it blinds me.
         (To them we are 'them'. More material for a thought.)

3.022.   Boys playing war, sleeves over hands, wallowing in boots.
         (Boys know the rules of the game.)

3.03.   At once everything stops.
         Blood looping in its orbits, its epicycles.

3.1.   Slow dawn. Ice on the river, my hand cramped on the switch.

                    A preliminary philosophy of war: solipsism is realism.
                       God says: you are a pious blueeyed killer, Ludwig.

3.2.   My duty is to peel this sack of potatoes. The grace of work!
         (Peeling potatoes for me is what lens-grinding was for Spinoza.)

3.3.   Afterwards I lie on the floor and read and write on a small wooden box.

3.31.   Tea, biscuits and chocolate, as if my mother had sent it, but no message.
         Is she dead? And why do they send me no message?

3.4.   A letter from David! I kiss it. I kiss it.
         He is not to fight! He is to fly, and in England too. I kiss it.

3.41.   His fingertips on the paper, his words, his lips, his breath.

3.42.   My comrades are beasts! Forgive me but they are beasts.

                       The soft lad has a letter from his English bumboy.
                          Him looking up at us, looking down his nose.

3.421. They stare through me. I am the form of a man merely.
I often cannot recognise the *human being* in a man.
(Bare beasts, brave beasts, rough beasts.)

3.43. The body is intractable, chaotic, it will not be led.
(We smell like dogs. We sleep like dogs.)

3.431. If God is one he is alone.
If God is two a third arises, as in the commerce of lovers,
their counterpoise.

3.44. Love is ferocious and war is tender.
Gunfire and ice. The Russians chase us back to Krakow.

3.5. Winter in the citadel. Orders and bells, black bread and wurst.

3.51. Christmas eve in a café, listening to the officers.
Paris has fallen! Paris has not fallen.
(Lemberg, though, is still in our hands.)

3.511. Doubt is foreign. Gott schütze Franz Josef!
Kirschwasser tossed back, cigars pinched and sucked, beaver
collars twitched up.
Silence.

God says: go back to your war.

3.6. My duty is to command the garrison forge. (Virtuous grease-monkey.)

3.61. My father's voice pounding in the hammers: the hard must, Ludi,
the hard must.
Doubled over, he weeps with laughter.

3.62. The barrel beaten down on the anvil, the sparks, the flaw, the blow.
I close my eyes. I wake in the infirmary.

3.7. I do not know and I cannot do.
And God will not say a word.

3.8. War becomes a way to go on living.
To go on living is a way of war.

Comfort me with tautologies.
Spare me age and second thought.
Reason me and beat me. Reduce me to my form.

4.   A toy train rolls across a map-table.

4.01.   Men propped like firewood, lulled by the sway and the rattle.
          We sleep and watch. We are carried east.

4.02.   At sunset the day begins, as dark as the inside of your belly.

4.021.   Looking out at my reflection, at the form of me, at nothing.

4.1.   Eastern nights are filled with forest.
          Ein Österreicher träumt vom Wald, so wie ein Engländer vom
          Meer träumt.
          (One cannot see far in the Wald.)

4.11.   Der Wald. *The* forest.
          Caesar in 'The Gallic Wars' says that one may walk east for sixty
          days and not reach the end of the Wald.

Waking into a dark wood, what do I see?

Birch and alder, beech and hornbeam. Eyes in the leaves.
I am born in a chaos of roots, carnage paused.

Carp and pike, hanging in columns of shade, flicking fins, watching.
The immense absence of a bull bison: hoofprints, turds, musk.

Cauldron bogs, dark and rancid, sated with bronze and bone.
Pagan thickets, hills of crosses. Bears and wolves dispute.
In a glade St Jerome reads to a lion.
In a shaft of sunlight I kneel before a stag.

The victors of Teutoburg feast on my carcass,
blowing raw notes from my flesh-tagged femur –

truces et caerulei oculi, rutilae comae,
magna corpora et tantum ad impetum valida

Tacitus dreams the Germans.
We dream endless east, empty east.

4.2.	Jarred awake, juddering over points. My head on the sergeant's shoulder.
	Breath on the glass. The stink of soldiers together.

4.21.	Shrouds of rain, falling but not here, hanging in the air, becoming.
	The raiments of an angel, not necessarily the angel of death.

4.211.	What grows on these light lands? Refugees.
	Bowed heads, raw feet, walking endless days, raped by God, by someone, anyway.

4.212.	An event occurs or does not occur, there is no middle course.
	(The syntax of a massacre.)

4.213.	Salted fields, splintered stone, the savour of death.
	(The dead are no wiser than the living.)

4.22.	What cannot be imagined cannot even be talked about.
	Though what is thinkable is also possible.
	(The sweet fatty scent of roasting lamb, the bitter herbs, the charoset.)

4.23.	Ritual is a way to go on.

4.231.	And so they go on dying and the dead live.

4.232.	They are not to blame for their sweet songs.
	(Passion, which denotes change.)

	God says: be fortunate in your ancestors.

4.3.	I am far from the heart of this.
	While there is light I read.

4.31.	Краткое Изложение Евангелия, the last book in the bookshop at Tarnow.

	He reads a Russian on the Gospel, that one,
		not a German nor an officer nor a man.

4.311.	Lyov Nikolayevich Tolstoy, holy innocent, sweetens my mouth.

The duty of life is only to exalt the Son of Man,
and the Son of Man exists always.

He is not in time; and therefore, in serving him,
one must live without time in the present alone.

4.32.   Light:

1. Christ on my breath, my tongue. Christ in my pulse, in my
    eyelashes, in the little bones of my throat.

2. Christ in a blue field coat, reading the gospel, on a train moving east.
    Christ eats black bread. Christ bites, chews, savours, swallows.
    (Christ is most monstrous when he eats.)

3. Christ as a peasant, digging in the fields. Christ thinks with his
    body, thinks of his father.

4. Christ shaves with the edge of a bayonet, webbed with frost.

5. Christ serves his father's gun, pistons seized, springs shrieking on pins.
    Christ as a shell in flight, blinded, rifled of pity, vengeful and precise.

6. Christ falls. Christ meets himself.
    Christ reaches down to me.
    (His hands, his strong breath.)

7. I am mastered. I am falling, over and over. Christ in my falling.
    Jerusalem.

God says: not yet.

Sitting there with his mouth hanging open.
Heathen. Schoolboy. Soft lad.

God says: no matter. Go on.

4.4.   The toy train jack-knifes, tumbles. Lead soldiers spill out.

4.41.   Officers in the high woods. Orders from textbooks.

4.411.   The success of an artillery assault depends upon precision: in mapping, in aiming, in observation.

4.412.   Each battery must register its own position, its observation posts, and its assigned targets.

4.4121.   Plane tables propped up in the dirt. Compass and slide rule, penknife and rubber, calculations done and redone. War is geometry and nothing more.

4.413.   A battery must be defiladed – hidden, that is, from enemy observation. Orchards are suitable for guns of small calibre, and the ruins of villages if the pieces are irregularly placed.

4.4131.   Mortars and howitzers unlimbered. Torn fingernails, handprints in oil, men harnessed like mules. Logs and turves piled up, heaped with brush.

4.414.   Shrapnel is particularly effective when the shells burst about twenty metres above personnel.
   A shell bursting in an enclosed space has a particularly violent effect.

4.4141.   Point fuse, graze fuse, delay fuse.
   Lethal gas, persistent gas, lachrymatory gas.
   Smoke shells, star shells, phosphorus.

                           Orders of angels. The work of grace!

4.5.   Six of us, down to braces and trousers, lined up, stiff, as for a photograph.
   Behind us our howitzer, snout up, snuffs the air, waiting.

4.51.   My duty is to cross this blue sky with shells.

Lay the shell, gently, on the cradle. Carry the cradle to the breech.
Work the shell into the chamber, ram it home, then the charge.
Lock the breech. Slot in the cap, attach the lanyard.
Check the elevation and the bearing. Check again.
All stand clear. Clear? Pull.

4.511.   Chemistry, then physics. Sound felt as a blow.
         The gun rolls back on its wedges, affronted, huffing.

4.5111. Again.

4.5112. Again.

4.5113. Again.

4.52.   Hard physical labour all day, many days; unable to think. Nights
         of flares and rumours.
            In the unit everyone hates me because no one understands me.
         And because I'm not a saint!

4.521.   Pray and wait. Your will be done.

4.6.   Thick coffee and black bread as the sun rises. Mist over the plain.
         Out of this silence something comes which leads us back to silence.

4.7.   At once everything happens –

4.71.   Red laughter. Concrete music.
         Bubbles of blast searching, sieving.
         Men winnowed down to blood and light.

4.72.   Dust in my eyes, shards of silence.
         We are their subjects. They reduce us to propositions.

4.721.   Two of ours open up. Russian shells keep falling.
         Bombardiers bellow into dead handsets.

                                              They've cut the line!

                   Wittgenstein! You're smallest. Get out to the forward OP
                             and don't come back without their corrections.

                                                      Your will be done.

4.73.   I am a shell, mortal, relentless, on the long curve of its life.

4.731.   Out of the battery, out of the camp, the track to the front. Two
         thousand metres in a moment.
            Blown, cartwheeling, into craters, drenched in dark water.
            I must not flinch. The hard must, screaming and twisting.

4.732.   Over the rifle pits, scumbling on chalk, on blood or something worse.

4.733.   Shell-hole to shell-hole, out to the OP, over the earthworks and in.

4.8.   Fire all around. The kingdom of heaven, bounded by death.
         The noise. The telephone screaming. Orders chanted in plainsong.

> MR 378268, El. 25° 30, FUZE 4.7, 5 Rds. RAPID
> Lift fire to that line of pollarded beeches.

4.81.   I am spirit and therefore I am free!
         O my soul. I am quick and dead, light as smoke.

4.811.   Here are new names for God: the bracketing salvo, the cloud of
         splinters, the body blown in three.
         Here is Christ in his blue field coat, his wounds, my comrade, my love.
         Here is everything required of me. Here is Jerusalem.

> God says: if you say so.
>
> He has volunteered for the OP, that runt.
> No more of him, then. A hermitage for a holy fool.
> You wish to go straight to the house of death, Wittgenstein?

5.   What lies beyond death is music.
     Music is the silence of heaven.

5.01.   A tune is a kind of tautology, it is complete in itself; it satisfies itself.
         We wait for resolution, kneeling.

5.011.   The shell, the blast, the crater; the instrument, the music, the musician.

5.1.   Freeze the shell in motion. Pluck it from the air.

5.11.   Loose skeins of geese, high above the plain.
         Moonlight smeared on chalk craters.

5.12.   Bodies tangled and determined, unhinged machines whispering:
ora et labora.
 Boys giving birth to their deaths.

5.13.   The present is a place to live. A tenancy.

5.2.   The world is the sum of these trajectories.

5.3.   Is a riddle solved by the fact that I live forever?
 For an answer which cannot be expressed the question too cannot
be expressed.
 The riddle does not exist.

5.31.   The limits of my language are the limits of my world, and the
limit of my world is death.
 (Mercy and pity in their parentheses, great suspended chords.)

5.32.   I am attuned, I am resonant, I shiver with harmony.

5.321.   He holds me between his knees, my head against his belly, his
long strong fingers fret the chords of my neck.
 We play, dutiful, wordless, the sarabande of the fifth cello suite.
 (The facts all belong to the task and not its performance.)

5.4.   Beyond death, beyond language, is this –

Volunteer Wittgenstein was attached to the Observer officer
during the engagements in front of Casemate JR77 (Cardinal Point
Saro) and the Cavalry Strongpoint Hill 458 from 4–6 June 1916.
Ignoring the heavy artillery fire on the casemate and the exploding
mortar bombs he observed the discharge of the mortars and located them.
The Battery in fact succeeded in destroying two of the heavy-calibre
mortars by direct hits, as was confirmed by prisoners taken. On the
Battery Observation Post, Hill 417, he observed without intermission
in the bombardment although I several times shouted to him
to take cover. By this distinctive behaviour he exercised
a very calming effect on his comrades.

5.5.   What is the distance, O Lord, between one moment and another?

God says: Who speaks?

Why is there something here
when there should be nothing?

5.51.   Faith in the action, not the word, the body, not the breath.
(To fall is to break, to speak.)

5.52.   Lanterns in the dark. The rivers up.
The skull of the moon, impact-polished, flesh-unsoftened.
A column of horses, silent, muscled, heads bowed like penitents.

They have broken through!
(Lemberg, though, is still in our hands.)

5.6.   The limits of my language mean the limits of my world and the
limit of my world is the road.

5.61.   The road is all that is the case.
Going on is all that is.
The howl of spent flesh is all.
(The banality of pain, its emptiness.)

5.62.   Happiness depends upon my realising the limits of the *sense* of
the world.
The sense of the world must lie outside the world.

No sense within.
Babbling into the dark like a child.

5.7.   We are children.
We do not *know* whether the sun will rise tomorrow.
(Is there comfort in this proposition, or sense?)

5.71.   Logic must take care of itself.
(God will not say: what kept you?)

5.711.   I am a compound noun in a picture-book alphabet:
ludwigsaddlereinshorseshoesroad.
     I ride a rocking horse. I wave a wooden sword. I triumph in
my nursery.

5.712.   A child knows how to go on.

5.72.   A stone, the body of a beast, the body of a man, my body, all
stand on the same level.
     My soul is my centre of gravity and no more. A failure of
nonexistence.

> God says: you will keep on, whether you want to
> or not, until you fall, whether you want to or not.

> This night more are trampled than picked off.
> You cowards! Stand and fight for your Emperor.

5.8.   They know how to go on.
     Stepping out of their rags, grinning, they join the retreat.

5.81.   Some march with us, some watch, some shuddered into monstrous
forms, some cuddled up as if asleep.

5.811.   The salivation of dead things – salvation, rather.
     The discourse of the dead, their squeaks, their intolerable dance.

5.812.   The equal self, unpicked, bone-bare. The name and nothing else,
or not even that.

5.813.   Paused in resurrection, palms out, gaping. We wait on them.

> Franz Josef ist tot!
> (Lemberg, though, is still in our hands.)

5.82.   Our emperor leads us!

5.821.   His whiskers tickle lipless teeth, his medals clink on ribs.
     He is master of the men who cannot bleed.

5.822.   Fräulein Todt on her pony, demure and hollow-hipped, raw sockets
behind her fan.
(Sloppy trombones, bass drum, Jews-harps.)

5.823.   We fall in after them. We know how to go on! We scream with joy.

5.9.   The world of the happy is quite another than that of the unhappy.

> I often think of you and ask myself
> how you are getting on. Please God
> we shall soon be able to play
> the *Winterreise* again.
> Ever your friend,
> Davy.

6.   He fell.

6.01.   His plane broke up. He fell five thousand feet.
(No space for parachutes.)

6.011.   Everything is happening at once.
He is falling and I am not holding him.
(Quite another world.)

6.0111.   Is there no domain outside the facts?

> Descending chords. A drunk hacks at the strings.

6.1.   Shall we meet in music?
We shall not meet in music.
We shall not meet.
He is falling and I am not holding him.
I throw myself after him.
I fight lithe death, his hide comes loose in handfuls.

6.11.   I reach after him. I am gravity's angel.
He clutches at the last rung. He slips.
(The agony of nothing called back to something.)
He is falling and I am not holding him.

6.12.   What is mirrored in language I cannot use language to express.
         If I have said everything I am left with the unspeakable.
         He is falling and I am not holding him.

                              Is there no domain outside the facts?

                                   Americans, now, and tanks.
                        (Lemberg, though, is still in our hands.)

6.2.   Salzburg station. Waiting for a train up into the Salzkammergut.
         (Lieutenant LJJ Wittgenstein, First Battery, Eleventh Mountain
         Artillery Regiment, Imperial and Royal Austro-Hungarian Army,
         Silver Medal for Valour, Military Merit Medal with Swords.)

6.21.   Tolstoy in my pocket, and a pistol.
         A sharper body than Davy ever knew.

6.22.   The express screams through. The noise!
         Out of the steam, on the platform beside me, Uncle Paul.

                                       Ludwig! You're alive.
                                       How are you, my boy?

6.221.   I'm alive, Uncle Paul, and this seems a failure.
         My first and only world is gone.
         My first and only friend has gone, and taken half my life with him.
         Between us a moment only and a leap – only a leap.

                        Just what this family needs: another corpse.
         Come with me to Hallein, Ludwig, and we'll sit by the stove and talk.

6.23.   There is so little left to say.

                                   Then we'll sit and be silent.

29

6.231.   What comes after the silence?

Life.

Ludwig, please don't die of devotion,
don't die of the hard must.
It achieves so little.

6.232.   How do you bear it? How do you go on?

A question without an answer.
I go on.

6.233.   I want to go on.
          Is it enough?

If this is all there is, it is more than enough.
Do you need to be told?

6.24.   Always.

Come to Hallein, Ludwig.
The sun will rise tomorrow if you will.
I'll buy the tickets. Let me carry your haversack.

God says: the good life is the life of wonder.

6.25.   The wonder of it.
          (The logical form of an angel, in a shabby sable coat.)

6.26.   I will learn to go on.

6.261.   I will learn to lack, to wait, to live by longing.

A preliminary philosophy of peace: longing is meaning.

6.262.   There is work for me, and grief.
           (A divine condition of not reaching.)

6.2621.   God requires my forgiveness and I his.

                    His ghost keeping distance, translucent with longing.

6.263.   Doubting has an end, but not yet.

6.27.   What can be said at all can be said clearly, and what is left to say
           is just this.

7.   The world is all that is the case –

                    everything we can and cannot bear.

Sources

The text behind this text is Wittgenstein's *Tractatus Logico-Philosophicus*, first published in English in 1922. I have used the 1961 edition, translated by DF Pears & BF McGuinness. For Wittgenstein's wartime experiences and ideas in his own words, I have drawn on his *Notebooks 1914–16*, edited by GH von Wright and translated by GEM Anscombe. Von Wright's *A Portrait of Wittgenstein as a Young Man: From the Diary of David Hume Pinsent, 1912–14* illuminates Pinsent's side of their relationship. 'Wittgenstein in the First World War' (wittgensteinchronology.com/wittgenstein-in-the-first-world-war-1914-1919) brought clarity to the chaos of the period. A full list of references to these and other primary sources may be found on my website – richardbarnettwriter.com.

Norman Stone's *The Eastern Front, 1914–1917* is still the most lucid short account of what EH Carr called 'the war no-one won'. The Imperial War Museum's 'Voices of the First World War' (iwm.org.uk/VoicesOfTheFirstWorldWar) brought the conflict movingly to life at its centenary. 'F.O.O.'s *With the Guns*, and *Artillery Firing*, an American translation of the French army's *Instruction sur le Tir d'Artillerie*, provide first-hand insights into the life and duties of a forward artillery observer (albeit an Allied one on the Western Front).

Anyone writing about Wittgenstein owes an immense debt of gratitude to Ray Monk. His biography, *Ludwig Wittgenstein: The Duty of Genius*, and his many shorter texts achieve what their subject called 'a proper ordering of experience and action'. Marjorie Perloff's *Wittgenstein's Ladder* is the locus classicus for reading the *Tractatus* as a poem. I also gained from Dominic Erdozain's *The Soul of Doubt*; Russell Hoban's ludicrously underrated *Pilgermann*; James C Klaage's *Wittgenstein in Exile*; Bryan McGuinness' *Wittgenstein: A Life: Young Ludwig 1889–1921*; Luigi Perissinotto's *The Darkness of This Time*; Nil Santiáñez's *Wittgenstein's Ethics and Modern Warfare*; Alexander Waugh's *The House of Wittgenstein* – and of course Derek Jarman's *Wittgenstein*, which brings laughter and joy to a subject so often overwhelmed by solemnity. Finally, Mark Fisher's *The Weird and the Eerie* suggested a way to write about silence.

The main character of this poem sometimes strays from the facts and the sequence of his biography. None of these sources should be held responsible; the deviations are deliberate and are all mine.

Notes

2.22. 'The hard 'Must', the hard 'Must'': a favourite phrase of Karl Wittgenstein, and something of an axiom amongst his sons.

3.51 & subsequently. 'Lemberg ist noch in unserem Besitz', the refrain of Karl Kraus' *The Last Days of Mankind*, 1918.

4.1. 'A German dreams of the forest, just as an Englishman dreams of the sea.'

Interjection after 4.11. 'Fierce blue eyes, red hair, huge frames, fit only for sudden exertion', from Caius Cornelius Tacitus, *De origine et situ Germanorum*, c. 98AD.

4.31. *The Gospel in Brief*: a chapter of Leo Tolstoy's *A Translation Harmony and Analysis of the Gospels*, 1892, published separately in 1902. Wittgenstein found a copy in Tarnow in 1914 – he said it was the last book left in the shop – and carried it throughout the war.

Interjection after 5.4. Wittgenstein's first citation for bravery, during the Brusilov offensive in June 1916.

Acknowledgements

I don't know what the late Michael Neve would have thought of this, but I wish he'd lived to read a poem that owes so much to his insight and his generosity of spirit. I'm grateful to Jessica Glueck for her attentive reading of the manuscript, to Tanera Bryden and Kate Ashton of the Nairn Book & Arts Festival for the opportunity to put some of the poem to an audience, and to Anna Halvares for weird and provoking exchanges on language and silence. Most of all I want to thank Lauren Jane Barnett, who knows that the good life is the life of wonder.